FLORENCE NIGHTINGALE

Published by
World Tribune Press
606 Wilshire Blvd.
Santa Monica, CA 90401

Design by Gopa & Ted2, Inc.
Cover image and page 39: Florence Nightingale Holding Lamp; page 2: Florence
Nightingale; page 13: Steel engraving of Florence Nightingale in hospital,
all © Bettmann/CORBIS.
Page 20: Florence Nightingale at work, © CORBIS
Page 33: Hospital at Scutari. Detail of Florence Nightingale at the ward, © Stapleton
Collection/CORBIS
Page 48: Florence Nightingale, © Hulton-Deutsch Collection/CORBIS

10 9 8 7 6 5 4 3 2 1

Florence Nightingale

IN TRIBUTE TO
THE CENTURY OF WOMEN

Daisaku Ikeda

World Tribune
Press

contents

Chapter 1   3

Chapter 2   11

Chapter 3   17

Chapter 4   31

Chapter 5   37

Chapter 6   45

Endnotes   53

Florence Nightingale

IN TRIBUTE TO THE CENTURY OF WOMEN

The twenty-first century is the century of life, the century
of health and the century of women. This is the story of
Florence Nightingale—a courageous woman who, as the pioneer
of an age of women, blazed bold new trails into uncharted
frontiers in the nineteenth century.

—January 2002

chapter 1

SHE WAS BORN into a wealthy upper-class family. She was loved by her family and those around her. She was raised in the lap of luxury. She was beautiful and well-educated. In fact, she was like a fairy-tale princess living in a golden castle on a lofty summit.

But this fairy-tale princess left her golden castle—overcoming the opposition of her family and friends—to aid those who were suffering. In a tumultuous era she lived and struggled with incredible strength, purity and pride, like a beautiful lotus flower blooming in a muddy pond. And she went on to forge a towering legacy of love for humanity that would inspire generations to come.

This woman was the founder of modern nursing, Florence Nightingale.

She was tender and caring, selfless and passionate, and had the sensitivity of a bodhisattva toward others' suffering and pain. She was cheerful, positive and compassionate. She was brave and unafraid of those in power. She was a person of immensely strong, unwavering conviction, and she was a person of action her entire life.

Her vibrant example truly reminds me of the women and young women of the Soka Gakkai's early days. And, of course, whenever I think of her life, a vision of our Soka Gakkai nurses groups appears before my eyes. I would like to express my deepest appreciation for our nurses' noble commitment to protecting the health and well-being of their fellow members by being constantly on standby to offer emergency medical assistance at various meetings and events.

I have spoken of Florence Nightingale on several occasions. I would like to focus on her life again, relating my thoughts as if in a warm-hearted conversation with the members of the women's and young women's divisions and our nurses groups members.

Early Life

Florence Nightingale was born on May 12, 1820, to wealthy British parents. When she was a girl, the family lived at Embley Park, a rambling country house in Hampshire, in the south of England. They spent the summers at Lea Hurst, their summer home in Derbyshire in central England, and resided in London during the social season.

Today there are not only many SGI members in London but also about 100 members in Hampshire. There are also members who are joyously carrying out activities in Derbyshire.

During Nightingale's time, England was at the forefront of the industrial revolution and London was the business capital of the world. The flourishing age of Queen Victoria was just beginning. At the same time, urban populations had exploded and a huge gap yawned between rich and poor. The living conditions of the poor were unspeakably wretched, and laborers were treated very badly. Typhus, cholera and other contagious diseases were endemic. This was the dark underside to the glittering life of the wealthy.

Nightingale was born on the outskirts of Florence, Italy. Immediately after their wedding, her parents set forth on a three-year honeymoon tour of the continent. Florence was their second child to be born on this extended honeymoon. She was named after the beautiful "City of Flowers."

There is also an SGI culture center in Florence today, and the Florentine members are busy creating a lovely flower garden of friendship in their community.

Nightingale's father was a graduate of Cambridge and a highly educated and cultured man. He was friends with the noted philosophers Jeremy Bentham (1748–1832) and John Stuart Mill (1806–73). Nightingale was educated by her father. She studied English composition and grammar; Latin, Greek, German, French and Italian; European history; and government, philosophy and mathematics. A governess instructed her in painting and music. This was an education far surpassing that usually given to women of her day.

Nightingale avidly absorbed it all. She read Plato, Dante and Goethe in the original languages. This remarkably broad course of study when she was young became the foundation that supported her activities as a citizen of the world in her adulthood.

Learning is a lifelong asset; it is the highway to the world.

Where Is Happiness?

Nightingale was raised in a loving, supportive family who held high expectations for her future. Attending balls in Paris and the theater in Italy, she seemed to be enjoying a glamorous and exciting youth. Her parents hoped that she would make a brilliant marriage, take her place in high society and live a life of perfect happiness. Her friends and acquaintances expected nothing less.

But something did not feel right to her.

Her relations with her large family first made her aware of the problem. At age 14, she had some 27 cousins, and they all wrote frequently and voluminously to each other about the smallest details of life—where they hoped to go on holiday, the selection of a new dress and so forth. This frivolous exchange disgusted the young Nightingale. Later she looked back on that time and wrote: "I craved for some regular occupation, for something worth doing instead of frittering time away on useless trifles."[1]

Material wealth could not fulfill the yearnings in Nightingale's heart. In fact, far from fulfillment, she felt a great inner void. From her late teens she continued to ask herself how to live a truly meaningful life and why she had been born into this world.

Suddenly one day Nightingale was confronted with the reality that her own world of ease was not shared by everyone else and that in fact the world was filled with pain and suffering. In the 1840s, England experienced a period of poor harvests and economic depression, a time that came to be called the "Hungry '40s." Nightingale first witnessed the piteous sight of farming families suffering from starvation and disease when she was 22. It was a tremendous shock for the sensitive young woman.

She wrote of her feelings: "My mind is absorbed with the idea of the sufferings of man, it besets me behind and before."[2]

When she complained to an aunt about the emptiness of their social life, the aunt replied that "even a dinner party could redound to the glory of God."[3] Nightingale retorted: "How can it be to the glory of God when there is so much misery among the poor, which we might be curing instead of living in luxury?"[4]

In her diary, she recorded her inner turmoil: "What is my business in this world?"[5] And she further observed: "Life is *not* a green pasture and a still water, as our homes make it."[6]

She could find nothing of satisfaction or interest in a life spent only in the pursuit of pleasures. In fact, she began to be repulsed by it. But she couldn't find the answer to her dilemma. Exhausted by her spiritual struggle, she tried to seek relief in travel.

The Questions of Life and Death

In the summer when Nightingale was 25 years old, her grandmother and her wet nurse fell seriously ill and Florence nursed them. As she cared for the sick, she began to feel revitalized. By working to help others, she was helping herself, she realized. On another occasion, she saw a poor sick woman die as the result of ignorance of those tending her, and she was outraged by the senselessness of such an unnecessary death.

Life and death—these are the hard questions of our existence. My mentor, second Soka Gakkai president Josei Toda, wrote as follows about the death of his beloved daughter: "I remember the suffering and anguish I experienced at the death of my infant daughter many years ago. At that time, I thought, I am so grief-stricken by her death, what would I do if my wife were to die? (My wife did die later, causing me great sorrow.) What would I do if my parents were to die? (They did in fact die, and I wept profusely.) When I asked myself those questions, I trembled. And when I contemplated being confronted with my own death, I felt dizzy and faint."

Then Mr. Toda advanced along the path of Buddhism. He later declared: "I have experienced life's hardships to the hilt. That is why I have been able to become the president of the Soka Gakkai."

The suffering of living. The suffering of aging. The suffering of illness. The suffering of death. No one can escape these things. The questions we must ask ourselves then are: how will we respond to life's harsh challenges? How will we leave some kind of record of our existence in this world?

Nightingale wrote: "A profession, a trade, a necessary occupation, something to fill and employ all my faculties, I have always felt essential to me. I have always longed for [this], consciously or not."[7]

She decided that her calling lay in devoting her life to nursing.

Nightingale realized that to help others required not only compassion and patience but also proper knowledge and training. In the winter of her 25th year, she announced to her family that she wanted to study nursing. They were fiercely opposed. Her older sister had a fit of hysterics. Her mother, who was always kind to those in need, was so overcome with fear and anger that she broke out in loud wails and sobs. "You are defiling yourself!" she cried. Even her progressive father did not understand her wishes.

Unlike the present, in those days nursing was regarded as an extremely lowly profession, and hospitals were despised places filled with foul odors and filth, lacking even the most rudimentary sanitary facilities. They were looked upon as places that bred immorality and vulgarity. Whenever anyone in the wealthy Nightingale family became ill, the doctor was summoned and they were treated in the comfort of their own home.

Florence Nightingale was anguished by her family's opposition, so much so that she herself fell ill. At last she had found her purpose in life, and now she was to be denied the opportunity to fulfill it!

Concealing her actions from her family, she would wake up early and study on her own—hospital organization and management, public health and other relevant subjects. Eventually she became as knowledgeable as any expert in the field.

At this time she wrote to a friend: "Life is no holiday game, nor is it a clever book, nor is it a school of instruction, nor a valley of tears; but it is a hard fight, a struggle, a wrestling [with] the Principle of Evil, hand to hand, foot to foot. Every inch of the way must be disputed."[8]

And she also declared resolutely: "Resignation! I never understood that word!"[9]

Life is a struggle! Florence Nightingale refused to give up. She was not defeated by prejudice or the lack of understanding from those around her. Her life struggle was to carry her through all sorts of suffering, one tenacious step at a time.

chapter 2

FLORENCE NIGHTINGALE first fully took up the challenge of nursing as a profession in her 30s. Declaring that she would have to *seize* what she needed to fulfill herself, because it would not be *given* to her,[1] she traveled to Germany to study at a special nursing school, with an attached hospital and orphanage. Life there was spartan. The work was demanding. But Nightingale took to it like a fish to water. She absorbed everything there was to know about nursing and excelled. That experience gave her, she wrote, "a feeling so brave as if nothing could ever vex me again."[2]

A strong inner conviction shines throughout Nightingale's life.

Once she decided on a course of action, her determination never wavered, no matter what obstacles she encountered. Even in her later years, when she had achieved so much and the world showered her with praise, she remained unchanged. She simply strove to do her best in everything she set out to accomplish. Appearances and personal vanity meant nothing to her.

Nightingale remarked on the folly of being overly influenced by what people said, by opinion, by external voices, adding that a sage had once noted: "No one has ever done anything great or useful by listening to the voices from without."[3]

What wisdom! What strength! Nothing can compare with those who remain true to themselves.

Buddhism teaches that the wise are not swayed by praise or censure, by the vagaries of public opinion.

Following a Lifelong Mission

Why was Nightingale able to build such a strong, unshakable self? I think it is because she embraced a noble calling, a mission. She cherished this sense of mission her entire life. "What is it to feel a *calling* for any thing?" she asked. "Is it not to do your work in it to satisfy your own high idea of what is the *right*, the *best*, and not because you will be 'found out' if you don't do it?"[4] This was her conviction.

For Nightingale, having a sense of mission was absolutely indispensable in the profession of nursing, which is committed to protecting the precious gift of life. For example, she wrote: "A nurse who has *not* such a 'calling,' will never be able to learn the sound of her patient's bell from that of others."[5] She passionately believed that without such total dedication one could not help those who were suffering and feeling anxious and alone.

A Buddhist scripture tells of Queen Shrimala of ancient India[6] coming before Shakyamuni Buddha and proclaiming her lifelong commitment to the bodhisattva way in the form of ten vows. One of those vows was to save all suffering living beings. The queen pledged: "When in the future I observe sentient beings who are friendless, trapped and bound, diseased, troubled, poor and miserable, I shall not forsake them for a single moment until they are restored."[7] She devoted her life to the practice of speaking kind words, giving alms, benefiting others and becoming one with those who needed help, earnestly striving to nurture the inherent good in people's lives.

Who are the women who are carrying out the practice of these noble vows in our world today? The members of the women's and young women's divisions who are chanting and working hard for the happiness of friends who are suffering and struggling with various problems. They are all noble bodhisattvas.

Nightingale stayed true to the path of her mission throughout her life. That was her greatness. It is a huge challenge to keep one's sense of mission burning brightly to the very end. How can we do this? Through unity, through solidarity with others who share our mission. Nightingale stressed the importance of "fostering that bond of sympathy (esprit de corps) which community of aims and of action in good work induces."[8] We must create an

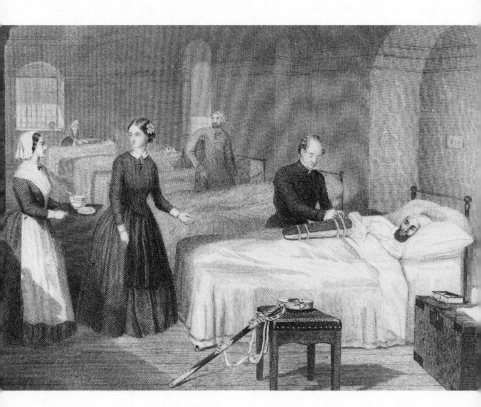

alliance of good that acts in solidarity and unity toward realizing a true, great goal—an alliance of like-minded individuals who have the strength of character to be true to themselves.

It is all very well to get by on our own when everything is going our way. But life is full of setbacks and unexpected difficulties. At such times, we shouldn't shut ourselves off from others. We should strive to encourage and support each other. "Let's challenge this together!" "Didn't we promise to win together?" "Let's have no regrets in life!" Mutual encouragement and support can be a source of great strength.

In addition, many people become lazy and complacent when they are spoiled and pampered and lack proper direction or challenges to help them grow. Those who lead such self-centered, self-indulgent lives are bound to veer from the path of happiness and end in powerless self-defeat. Nightingale wisely realized this fact of human nature.

Training in Our Youth Is the Treasure of a Lifetime

Nichiren Daishonin writes: "A person of considerable strength, when alone, may fall down on an uneven path. . . . Therefore, the best way to attain Buddhahood is to encounter a good friend" (*The Writings of Nichiren Daishonin*, p. 598). Herein also lies the significance of Tsunesaburo Makiguchi and Josei Toda founding the Soka Gakkai in order to launch their struggle for kosen-rufu. Mr. Toda even boldly proclaimed, "The Soka Gakkai organization is more precious than my own life."

An American scholar who is an SGI-USA leader once asked me: "How can we advance on the right path and fulfill our mission without any wasted effort?" I replied that one crucial point is never to detach ourselves from the SGI—the organization of faith and kosen-rufu that upholds the Mystic Law of cause and effect. No matter what happens, it is important that we live and strive together with the SGI and our fellow SGI members throughout our lives.

How crucial and heartening the presence of our organization is!

In every arena of life, if we try to avoid engagement with other people and groups and get by entirely on our own, more often than not we become self-indulgent and egotistic. If we let ourselves be swept away by circumstances and forget and abandon our own noble mission, we are living lives that, though they may seem free, are ultimately the most confining of all.

The SGI provides us with encouragement, training and opportunities for self-improvement. By actively striving as part of the SGI, we can build an unshakable foundation of happiness.

Nightingale was well aware of the importance of people inspiring each other and helping each other grow. In her later years, she wrote to a friend: "To live your life, you must discipline it. You must not fritter it away in 'fair purpose, erring act, inconstant will.'"[9]

The training we undergo in youth is the treasure of a lifetime.

chapter 3

I HAVE HAD THE PLEASURE of meeting with Ukraine's Ambassador to Japan Yuriy Kostenko and his wife, Dr. Liudmyla Skyrda. During our conversation, the ambassador mentioned the beauties of the Crimean Peninsula, proudly calling it one of the loveliest spots in the world. This beautiful place, however, became the scene of a bloody conflict, the Crimean War (1853–56).

The Black Sea is located to the south of Russia. Having won a war against Turkey, Russia gained access to the Black Sea. This alarmed England and France, and they urged Turkey to strike back. In 1853, Turkey declared war on Russia. The conflict soon developed into a major war with an alliance of England, France, and Turkey fighting against Russia. The Crimean Peninsula, where most of the fighting took place, is now part of Ukraine.

The alliance eventually lost 70,000 soldiers and Russia 130,000. Leo Tolstoy, then in his 20s, was an officer in the Russian forces during the war and was stationed at Sebastopol, site of one of the bloodiest battles. He wrote several short stories based on his wartime experiences, including "Sebastopol in December."

Tolstoy soon realized that there was nothing heroic or glorious about war. It was filled with bloodshed, suffering and death. This horrific experience was to be a formative one in the youthful Tolstoy's life; his direct observation of the folly of war ultimately led him to the absolute pacifism of his later years.

The Misery of War

It is always the nameless ordinary people who are the greatest victims of war. I was in my teens during World War II, and I still remember the sight of an elderly couple fleeing in terror during a nighttime bombing raid and a group of men, apparently of some social standing, quaking with fear as they ran for cover. My eldest brother, whom I dearly loved and respected, died in the fighting in Burma (now Myanmar). I can still picture my mother when she received the news of his death, her back turned from us, her shoulders shaking as she tried to suppress her tears.

How many mothers and fathers wept tears of grief at the loss of their young sons whose futures they had looked forward to with such hope? How many people were separated forever from their husbands, their sweethearts? The war cast untold ordinary citizens into the depths of unhappiness.

I was suffering from a lung disease at the time. I will never forget the remarks of a middle-aged nurse who came to my assistance: "War is awful, isn't it? I hope it ends soon." At a time when the whole nation was mobilized toward the war effort, those were very brave words indeed.

Now we the members of the SGI are pressing forward toward the goal of humanism—to put the war-racked twentieth century forever behind us and create a twenty-first century of peace without fail.

When Florence Nightingale read newspaper accounts of the enormous death rate of the wounded and sick soldiers on the Crimean front because of a lack of proper medical treatment, she was appalled and driven to take action. Having completed her course of nursing training in Germany, she was working as the head of the nursing department at a London hospital. Now she began to make preparations to go to the battlefront with a group of nurses at her own expense. Her family opposed her decision.

Just at that time, the British Secretary of War was considering sending nurses to the front lines, and he selected Nightingale to lead this undertaking. The government then made an official request that she go and assist the wounded. This brought about a major change in her family's attitude.

With a group of thirty-eight nurses, Nightingale headed for the battlefront. On her departure her mother sent her, for the first time, a letter of congratulations. It was October 1854, and she was thirty-four.

Nightingale was assigned to a British military hospital located in Turkey. The conditions at this facility were horrendous beyond imagination. There were far more patients than the hospital could handle, and they were crammed together in any space available in the wards. There was insufficient food, water and fuel, and even essential medical equipment and medicines were lacking. It was also filthy, overrun with rats, lice and germs. Wounded soldiers were more likely to die from cholera, typhus and other diseases caused by the unsanitary conditions than of their injuries. It was a deplorable tragedy, and as head of the nursing staff, Nightingale found herself thrown into the midst of it. A grand struggle that would last two years had begun.

Persevering with Patience and Determination

What was the first obstacle she faced? Arrogant military doctors and officers who were openly prejudiced against nurses and viewed them with contempt. They had opposed the dispatch of the nursing team, declaring that the women were interfering in men's work and would be of no use. To them, the nurses were nothing but a nuisance.

The treatment of the nurses was abominable. For their quarters, the thirty-eight nurses were assigned a kitchen and five small rooms, one of which was a closet, which Nightingale ultimately made her quarters.

The doctors patently ignored them. For days Nightingale and her nurses weren't even allowed to enter the wards because the doctors hadn't granted permission. Why on earth had they come? they asked themselves.

But Nightingale was patient. She had a mission to accomplish. "The consideration of overwhelming importance," she wrote, "was the opportunity offered to advance the cause of nursing.... If the nurses acquitted themselves creditably, never again would they be despised."[1] This was the determination that kept her going.

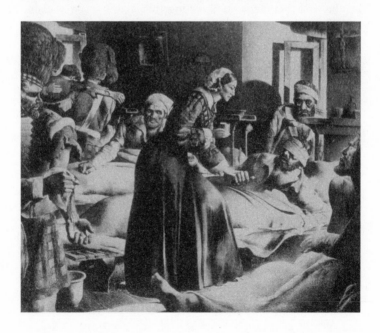

Nightingale decided not to cause unnecessary friction but to try to win the trust of the doctors and officers. She and the nurses made pillows and bandages. They prepared meals. They actively sought out things that needed doing and set themselves diligently to them.

The war took a turn for the worse, and wounded soldiers came flooding into the hospital. Some of them were Russians. The hospital was stretched beyond its capacities. Finally, the doctors approached Nightingale and asked for her assistance.

She threw herself heart and soul into the task of nursing, working with utter devotion from early in the morning to far into the night, often without resting. She never left the hospital for even a moment. She also assisted at major surgeries and often remained on her feet for twenty hours and longer dressing wounds and sores.

The more serious a patient's condition, the more diligently she cared for him. She did everything in her power to lessen her patients' suffering. She was always there at the bedside of the dying. One of the doctors wrote, with astonishment and praise: "I believe that there was never a severe case of any kind that escaped her notice, and sometimes it was wonderful to see her at the bedside of a patient who had been admitted perhaps an hour before, and of whose arrival one would hardly have supposed she could be already cognisant."[2]

She was determined that no patient who came into her sight, regardless of who they were, would feel deserted or alone. As she made her rounds of the wards, she would speak kindly to the men, smile and lay a gentle hand on them, encouraging each one. What a tremendous source of comfort this must have been for the soldiers!

Whenever there was a crisis, Nightingale was there—so much

so that the soldiers began to say that there must be more than one of her.

Nightingale was always cheerful in front of the patients, no matter how busy she was or how trying her situation. She was always filled with energy. She didn't lose her sense of humor. She emanated an aura of caring and compassion. Her lively demeanor and cheerful voice was a fountain of hope to the dispirited patients.

Before Nightingale arrived at the hospital, there had been an unceasing stream of complaints, curses and unpleasantness. Gradually, a new mood of peacefulness and purity filled the wards. Under Nightingale's influence, soldiers promised to give up drinking and to send money back to their families.

When one woman stands up for a cause, what a momentous impact she can have on those around her!

Nightingale, who came to be known as "the Angel of the Crimea," not only helped mend the physical wounds of those in her care but revitalized spirits that had been hardened and calloused by the war.

In her later years, she wrote: "The Angels are they who, like Nurse or Ward-maid or Scavenger, do disgusting work, removing injury to health or obstacles to recovery, emptying slops, washing patients, etc., for all of which they receive no thanks.... The drabby Nurse, crying as if her heart would break, with apron over her head, because a poor little peevish thing who has never given her anything but trouble is dead—is an Angel."[3]

I am reminded of a famous anecdote about Shakyamuni from the Buddhist scriptures. There was a sick man who had been abandoned by all—all, that is, except Shakyamuni, who reached out to help him. He stroked the man gently, washed his soiled body and even changed his bedding. He nursed him devotedly.

Some of Shakyamuni's followers asked why the Buddha was doing this. Shakyamuni replied: "If you wish to serve the Buddha, tend the sick."

The Buddha taught that there are illnesses of the body and illnesses of the mind, and we must do everything in our power to heal them. It is important that we care for those who are sick as if they were the Buddha. Buddhist practice exists only in struggling in the midst of humanity.

With Lamp in Hand

Nightingale's work went on late into the night when all else were asleep. At night, she applied herself to a mountain of correspondence. In a single winter, she was present at the deathbeds of more than 2,000 patients, and with immense thoughtfulness she wrote letters to their mothers and wives, describing the men's last moments and sharing their final words and expressions of love for their families. These letters, filled with sympathy and kindness, were like beacons of light that helped the survivors overcome their grief.

She also received many letters from mothers and wives inquiring about their sons and husbands, and she personally answered each one. When a concerned bystander, fearing for her health, urged her to rest, she said it was impossible, as she had far too many letters to reply to, pointing to a stack on her desk. When asked why she didn't leave them until tomorrow, she answered that tomorrow she had tomorrow's work to do.

Nightingale's work went on to one or two o'clock in the morning, and sometimes even later, to three or four o'clock. It wasn't rare for her to go without any sleep at all. Also late every night, after all the doctors had long retired to their quarters, she made a round of the wards. She walked softly through the stillness with a small lantern in hand, going from ward to ward, observing her patients with a careful eye. This was her nightly practice.

Word of her devotion was conveyed by the letters the soldiers sent home, and her reputation grew, not only in England but across the globe. The American poet Henry David Longfellow dedicated a poem to her:

Lo! in that hour of misery
A lady with a lamp I see
Pass through the glimmering gloom,
And flit from room to room.
And slow, as in a dream of bliss,
The speechless sufferer turns to kiss
Her shadow, as it falls
Upon the darkening walls.[4]

No one told her to make night rounds of the wards or to undertake the heavy task of writing letters to soldiers' relatives. They were expressions of her sense of mission and duty as head nurse. Nightingale valued a sense of duty and responsibility very highly. For example, many times major accidents are caused by small oversights. The reason for such events, she said, were clear: "[It is] simply because no one seemed to know what it is to be 'in charge,' or who was in charge."[5] She also wrote, "Of all human sounds, I think the words I don't know are the saddest."[6] She was always strongly aware of what she must do.

A deep sense of responsibility produces wisdom and strength and expands one's state of life. The various positions in our organization for kosen-rufu are not just titles, either. They are positions of responsibility and are a noble tradition of the SGI.

The number of the wounded continued to grow. Nursing them was challenging enough, but Nightingale also had the additional responsibility of the practical day-to-day managing and running of the hospital. It was incredibly demanding. She cooked, washed, cleaned and received visitors to the hospital. She had to keep records of a huge quantity of donated gifts and write thank-you letters, requisitions and official reports. Describing her work in Crimea, she wrote, "Nursing is the least of the functions into which I have been forced."[7]

She used her own funds to purchase food, clothing and personal items for the patients. She also organized new kitchens, reading rooms and classes and lectures for the convalescing soldiers. At her suggestion, facilities such as a dissecting room for postmortem examinations were built. It was said that without her, the hospital would have completely ceased to function. Her work was indeed magnificent.

Obstructed by the Apathetic and Devious

Why was Nightingale forced to bear this tremendous burden on her own? She wrote to one of her supporters back in England, "The real humiliation, the real hardship of this place . . . is that we have to do with men who are neither gentlemen nor men of education nor even men of business, nor men of feeling, whose only object is to keep themselves out of blame."[8]

An attitude of apathy and irresponsibility was prevalent everywhere in the hospital. The highest ranking military doctor felt that his assignment to Crimea was a demotion, and he cared little about doing a good job. He negligently reported back to England that the hospital was running smoothly and they were well supplied. The real situation was disclosed by the reports sent back by

Nightingale. She wrote to political leaders in England, boldly stating the truth and fearlessly criticizing where criticism was due. Making them her allies, she carried out reform after reform at the hospital.

Conservative forces who believed that women should keep out of the war and medical treatment in general marveled at her strong will and decisive actions and called them manifestations of "Nightingale power."

The military doctor in charge of the hospital was jealous of Nightingale. He obstructed her every move and attacked her with every means at his disposal. The British military command in Crimea also regarded her as an adversary, because she fearlessly reported the true situation of the wounded soldiers to the government. When these military leaders heard reports of the praise and applause she was receiving back in England, they redoubled their devious efforts to undermine her. She wrote, "There is not an official who would not burn me like Joan of Arc if he could, but they know the War Office cannot turn me out because the country is with me—that is my position."[9]

First Soka Gakkai president Tsunesaburo Makiguchi said: "Unless you have the courage to be an enemy of those who are evil, you cannot be a friend to the good."[10] If we struggle in earnest for justice and good, we will inevitably incur jealousy, hostility and persecution from evil people. This is a constant of history. Only those who can calmly and resolutely triumph over such obstacles are people of true courage and genuine victors in life.

Nightingale was extremely thoughtful and considerate of others.

Many of the nurses dispatched with her to Crimea were inexperienced. In fact, they were more of an encumbrance than a help, yet Nightingale sincerely respected and valued them. She went so far as to ask her mother and sister in England to visit the nurses' families and reassure and encourage them. Though at the start her mother and sister had so vehemently opposed her choice of a career, now they gladly agreed to assist her.

Nightingale also wrote letters to the nurses' families, describing their circumstances. She spared no effort behind the scenes to make it possible for her coworkers to do their best.

In spite of this, some of the nurses gave up and returned home, complaining that the rules were too strict or that they didn't like the nursing caps they had to wear. Some grumbled that they weren't allowed to do the kind of work they wished to. One of the nurses, filled with spite, even went so far as to spread groundless rumors back in England, claiming that Nightingale was deliberately starving patients to death.

A second group of nurses was sent to Crimea, and their leader openly opposed Nightingale. She zealously tried to show that she could do a better job. Out of envy for Nightingale's reputation, she caused dissension among the nurses and hindered their work. But Nightingale knew that jealous people bring more harm to themselves than others.

And in fact, when this jealous nurse was appointed to head of another hospital, she was revealed as incompetent and fell into a panic. She and the nurses under her direction refused to get their own hands dirty, and a large number of wounded soldiers died as a result. Unable to manage the hospital, she returned to England in ignominious defeat.

Nightingale's struggle paid off and the hospital under her charge began to run smoothly—at which point the officials and doctors immediately forgot the debt they owed her and began to disregard her. Though they had listened to her advice up to now, they began to stop consulting her. Worse, they attacked her, baselessly accusing her and her nurses of being extravagant and wasteful. She was surrounded by foes on all sides.

Then an even more serious event occurred. The nurse that Nightingale had placed in charge of the donated gifts was found to have stolen a large quantity of them. To avoid a scandal, Nightingale quietly sent the woman back to England. Once home, instead of being grateful for the kind treatment she had received, the woman caused an uproar, claiming that it was Nightingale herself who had appropriated the donations for private use. She even went so far as to take legal action in an effort to place the blame for her actions on Nightingale, repaying the latter's consideration and tact with enmity.

It was an incredibly stupid course of action.

But Nightingale was not cowed. She did not give in to despair or self-pity. This was because she never forgot her patients, who were as dear to her as her own children. She never for an instant forgot her mission to protect and aid the sick and wounded.

History proved Nightingale's complete innocence of the slanderous charges, while the malicious woman who leveled the false accusations merely ensured that she would earn eternal scorn for her deeds from later generations.

Actions Pervaded by a Great Vow

Nightingale even went to the front lines, where the fighting raged furiously. She visited hospitals there and also the trenches.

She collapsed on this trip, struck by deadly Crimean fever. It was as if the floodgates had suddenly opened and all the grueling hardships she had thus far experienced finally caught up with her. She was utterly exhausted, both physically and mentally. She almost died and even the doctors despaired of her recovery. When the hospitalized soldiers learned of her grave condition, they turned their faces to the wall and wept.

For more than two weeks Nightingale remained in a critical condition, but even then she did not give up her struggle. Though delirious with fever, she refused to put down her pen, continuing to write out instructions and requisitions and to keep lists. Working and struggling had penetrated into the very depths of her being.

Perhaps because of her invincible determination, she recovered miraculously. But she had used her body so strenuously that she never fully regained her health. She was afflicted with painful rheumatism and sciatic neuralgia and had to be hospitalized again. Still she refused to listen to those who urged her to return to England. She declare, "I have now had all that this climate can give, Crimean fever, Dysentery, Rheumatism and believe myself thoroughly acclimatised and ready to stand out the war with any man."[11]

When the Crimean War came to an end in March 1856 with the signing of a peace treaty in Paris, Nightingale set to work finding jobs for her nurses after their return to England. She would not allow them to be "discarded like worn-out shoes." One after another, the nurses left for home, but Nightingale stayed behind, "as long as a nurse could be of some use." She continued her duties until July, leaving only after the last wounded soldier was sent home. She finally returned to England in August, having carried out all of her responsibilities to the very end.

A life of unceasing struggle is beautiful. A life of continual advance is invigorating.

Nightingale's actions were pervaded by a great vow, which allowed her to remain unperturbed by the petty jealousies and foolish behavior of others.

Our goal is kosen-rufu. As long as the core of that great purpose remains strong and steady within us, nothing in life will be able to shake us.

Nightingale reflected on the senseless deaths of so many young men in the Crimean War, and after returning to England, she began a new struggle to protect life and health. She wrote, "If I could only carry one point which would prevent one part of the recurrence of the colossal calamity; then I should be true to the brave dead."[12]

Eight years later, in 1864, Jean Henri Dunant founded the International Red Cross, inspired, it is said, by Nightingale's nursing during the Crimean War.

chapter 4

In the middle of war, Florence Nightingale took decisive steps to improve the appalling conditions at military hospitals. She also made it her mission to revolutionize the profession of nursing, succeeding in elevating the once lowly position of nurses to such an extent that they became known as "ministering angels."

All of England was excited at the return of Nightingale, their new national hero. A tumultuous chorus of praise greeted her. Yet she accepted all this sudden applause for her work as a nurse as an irksome burden. Why? Because she believed that "the small, still beginning, the simple hardship, the silent and *gradual* struggle upwards; these are the climate in which an enterprise really thrives and grows."[1]

Things easily achieved are also easily destroyed. An unshakable foundation leading to eternal glory is built through steady progress, as natural and gradual as the flow of water; it is achieved one step at a time, overcoming various hardships and working quietly and inconspicuously. This is also how the Soka Gakkai has advanced and the reason why we have developed to the extent we have today.

Continued efforts, sincerity and patience—these are the source of the Soka Gakkai's strength, achievements, and propelling force.

The Real Struggle Is Yet to Come!

The long conflict in Crimea was over, and people wished to forget the disreputable war as quickly as possible. For Nightingale, however, the struggle was not over. She resolved to fight on, fully recognizing that her real struggle was yet to come.

Her experience in Crimea led her to the conclusion that nursing itself must be reformed. Had there been a properly established nursing system in place, she felt, many more precious lives could have been saved in Crimea. She refused to let the deaths of the sick and wounded be in vain. Soon after returning home she wrote: "I stand at the altar of the murdered men, and while I live I fight their cause."[2]

Some urged Nightingale to rest and recuperate. True, she was indeed exhausted after her grueling exertions, but she believed she needed to take action while the memory of the tragedy of the war was still fresh in people's mind. She wanted to strike while the iron was hot. Spurring herself on, she set to work again. Forward, ever forward, never looking back. The past was the past, and the future lay ahead. In this spirit of continual advance, we can see Nightingale's greatness. She would not permit herself to remain still. Until her death at age 90, Nightingale continued her struggle without ceasing, without compromise.

The example of Nightingale reminds me of the indomitable spirit of world-renowned physicist Joseph Rotblat. At 93, Dr. Rotblat is president emeritus of the Pugwash Conferences on Science and World Affairs and a recipient of the 1995 Nobel Peace Prize. He is internationally acclaimed for his contributions to science and humanity. I will never forget him telling me proudly that he didn't allow himself to be tired.

President Josei left us with the injunction: "Never slacken in your struggle against evil." We must fight on resolutely and without rest. We must never stop. This is the secret to health and eternal victory; it is also the way to complete the drama of our human revolution.

Nightingale's struggle for health reform was not limited to public health but extended to political and economic issues as well, even later reaching countries outside England.

To improve the treatment of soldiers, she pushed political leaders to revamp Britain's War Office. She worked industriously to

reform laws for protecting people's health, such as the Poor Law. In addition, when Nightingale learned of the appalling sanitary conditions of the soldiers and peasants in India, which was then a British colony, she poured her energy into rectifying that situation as well.

Any one of these was a formidable undertaking for a single individual to tackle. They presented even greater obstacles than Nightingale had faced in Crimea. Her life became a series of fierce and tortuous struggles.

She once spoke to a statistician. She wanted to compare the rates of sickness and death of those living in military barracks with those of ordinary civilians. By presenting actual figures, she hoped to impress on people just how dreadful the conditions in the barracks were. The statistician warned her that if she pursued such a course of action she would make many enemies. But Nightingale replied resolutely that after everything she had seen in the war she could fire her own guns of conviction now.[3]

Life had taught her to have the strength to be fearless in the face of difficulties and to refuse to retreat a single step, under any circumstance. She had no patience for big talkers, no matter how eloquent, who took no action. She said: "Don't let us be like the chorus at the play which cries 'Forward, forward' every two minutes and never stirs a step."[4]

This is indeed a characteristic statement of Nightingale, who set an example by always taking action herself.

A Prolific Writer

Nightingale also became a prolific author. She wrote many books and papers, for the sake of future generations.

In 1859 she published her *Notes on Hospitals*, proposing hospital reform. Then she published her famous *Notes on Nursing: What It Is, and What It Is Not,* in which she discussed the proper approach to nursing and the knowledge required to safeguard health. She also published philosophic and religious works such as *Suggestions for Thought to the Searchers after Truth among the Artizans of England.* In addition, she wrote a number of books on India, including *Suggestions on a System of Nursing for Hospitals in India* (1865) and *Life or Death in India* (1874). She also wrote works such as *Suggestions on the Subject of Providing, Training, and Organising Nurses for the Sick Poor in Workhouse Infirmaries* (1867), *Introductory Notes on Lying-in [Maternity] Institutions* (1871), *Health Teaching in Towns and Villages* (1894), and many others, numbering nearly 200 publications in all.

Books have enormous power. Good books that are infused with the authors' heart and soul can transcend borders and spread around the world, transcending time and shining with eternal brilliance. Incidentally, overseas visitors frequently astonish me by saying they have been reading my works for decades.

Of all Nightingale's writings, *Notes on Nursing* provoked the greatest response. The book contains profound insights about health and disease. What is illness? She argues: "All disease, at some period or other of its course, is more or less a reparative process, not necessarily accompanied with suffering: an effort of nature to remedy a process of poisoning or of decay."[5]

She did not have a tragic or negative view of illness. She knew that sickness and health were inseparable and apprehended illness dynamically as a function of the body's natural healing powers.

I have published a dialogue with leading cancer researcher Dr. René Simard (former rector of the University of Montreal), and noted bioethicist Dr. Guy Bourgeault (professor at the same university). [*The book,* On Being Human, *originally published in*

*Japanese and French, will be available in September 2003 as a
paperback edition from Middleway Press.]*

In that dialogue, Dr. Bourgeault stated that health is neither an
absence of illness nor simply a stable state: "Essentially, good
health is less the absence of illness than the tension between a
precarious equilibrium and the constant dynamic of its reestab-
lishment."

This is expressed in Buddhism as the oneness of health and illness. Buddhism teaches that in confronting illness and fighting
toward recovery—both in the case of ourselves and others—we
strengthen our natural healing powers and gain true mental and
physical health.

Health is a universal wish. We need to build a 21st century
where all humanity and human society shine with good health.

Eiichi Yamazaki, our late SGI-Europe honorary chairperson,
was a doctor of medicine. He placed a copy of my dialogue with
the Canadian scholars by his bedside the night before he died,
intending to start translating it the next day. In the past an American research team had strongly urged Dr. Yamazaki to join them
in their work. The team later won a Nobel Prize. But Dr. Yamazaki
turned down their request, saying that he wanted to devote his
life to spreading the Daishonin's teachings in Europe and to sup-
porting his fellow members, and he remained in France. He gave
his life to the propagation of the Mystic Law. He is an example to
all members of the doctors' division.

Today, doctors of the Mystic Law are spreading their wings of
mission throughout the world. I would like to eternally honor
their noble lives.

chapter 5

ILLNESS IS PAINFUL. However, the suffering and pain associated with illness is not necessarily caused by the illness itself, observed Florence Nightingale, but by something quite different: "the want of fresh air, or of light, or of warmth, or of quiet, or of cleanliness, or of punctuality and care in the administration of diet, of each or of all of these. And this quite as much in private as in hospital nursing."[1]

The sick person's environment is very important. Nightingale realized that though the patient might be heading toward physical recovery, without proper attention and nursing skill to support the healing process, recovery could be obstructed, resulting in pain and suffering, or in fact even halted.

Nursing up to this time had been little more than dispensing medicine, and it was thought that all nurses needed to know was how to mix plasters and poultices. Nursing was looked down upon as something anyone could do, without study or training.

Nightingale revolutionized society's view of nursing. She argued: "[Nursing] ought to signify the proper use of fresh air, light, warmth, cleanliness, quiet, and the proper selection and administration of diet—all at the least expense of vital power to the patient."[2] Elsewhere she said: "Nursing is therefore to help the patient to live."[3]

She set forth what nursing should be from a patient's point of view, illuminating the issue from every angle. This no doubt arose from her compassionate nature, which constantly directed its attention to how she could alleviate suffering. She elevated nursing to an art requiring practical and scientific training—one that humanity should devote serious attention to. This is why she is known as the founder of modern nursing.

Tsunesaburo Makiguchi tried to carry out a similar revolution in the field of education.

Both medicine and education deal with human life. In the field of medicine, a scientific framework had been formed and principles for training people in medical techniques had come to be established. In contrast, the field of education remained largely governed by abstract theories. Mr. Makiguchi lamented this fact, insisting that education must develop a systematic approach comparable to that of medicine.

His system of value-creating education was the culmination of his fervent wish to carry out a fundamental reform of education, to break through the impasse that afflicted all society and to help suffering children. He believed that education was the "supreme human science and art of creating the value of character."

Nursing That Strengthens Life Force

Nightingale vigorously advocated the importance of fresh air and sunlight, a very progressive view for her time. The hospitals of the day fell far short of modern standards of hygiene. They lacked adequate sanitary facilities and good ventilation. To keep the rooms warm, the windows were kept tightly shut. And the beds were arranged in such a way that no sunlight should fall on them. Some hospitals even nailed boards over the windows to keep the sun out. As a result, hospital rooms were always dark and damp.

Nightingale threw open those windows and taught the healthful effects of sunlight.

How can people's vital life force be strengthened? Buddhism teaches "the oneness of life and its environment" and "the oneness of the universe and the self." In its inner reality, our life is one with the natural environment and the universe itself. Living in harmony with nature strengthens our innate life force.

The Lotus Sutra also contains the principles of "perennial youth and eternal life" and of "prolonging one's life through faith." "Life" here can be interpreted as "life force." When we chant the Mystic Law with a resounding voice an ever-youthful life force will rise up powerfully within us.

What is important in building hospitals for patients? In the introduction to her *Notes on Hospitals*, Nightingale wrote: "It may seem a strange principle to enunciate as the very first requirement in a Hospital that it should do the sick no harm."[4] This book contains many insights into hospital buildings, including their functions and facilities. From her rich fund of experience, Nightingale writes in detail about structure, building materials for ceilings, walls and floors and even the color the walls should be painted.

In June 1994, I was invited to the private estate of His Royal Highness Prince Charles of the United Kingdom, and we enjoyed an extended discussion on the topic of the need to restore human values and a human face to contemporary civilization. The subject of hospital architecture also came up. Prince Charles is well-versed in architecture and, in a book he wrote on the subject, he makes the observation: "It can't be easy to be healed in a soulless concrete box with characterless windows, inhospitable corridors and purely functional wards. The spirit needs healing as well as the body."[5] He also said: "I believe that it is most certainly possible to design features which are positively healing in such buildings."[6]

I agree. When I quoted these passages of his book to the prince, he smiled appreciatively.

As society ages, proper care of the elderly is becoming a subject of growing concern. Nightingale's philosophy of nursing continues to offer valuable suggestions for us today. Indeed, it is very close to the Buddhist concept of nursing based on compassion.

According to Buddhism, the causes of human suffering are not necessarily limited to physical pain. In other words, human suffering is viewed as a composite of physical pain, psychological, spiritual and social suffering and also existential suffering arising from having to confront the reality of death.

Nightingale held the same view. How could patients be relieved of their sufferings? How could they be encouraged and emotionally supported? She remarked that it was commonly thought that nurses were there to free patients from physical exertion, whereas in fact they ought to be there to free patients from needless fretting and worrying.[7] Nightingale expanded the boundaries of nursing to include treating psychological and social suffering as well.

Nightingale's Devotion to Educating Nurses

As a means of developing the nursing profession, Nightingale placed great value on education. She fostered many young people in this field. At her instigation, a training school for midwives was opened at the famous King's College Hospital in London.

The Nightingale Training School for Nurses at Saint Thomas's Hospital in London was opened on June 24, 1860. Nightingale founded the school with the Nightingale Fund, comprising donations received from the public in support of her efforts. She was 40 at the time.

With her continuing fragile health and being kept extremely busy with various issues, for a long time she was unable to personally visit the school. Nevertheless, as its founder, she rejoiced at the realization of her long-cherished dream of a facility for the education and training of nurses. As one of her biographers noted: "She wanted to sow an acorn which might in course of time produce a forest."[8] With this spirit, Nightingale watched over the school all her life.

The first class had an enrollment of fifteen students. This small group of talented, carefully selected students was given intensive instruction and training. Nightingale read the students' reports, daily journals, test papers and lecture notes. She enjoyed nothing more than observing their vigorous growth. On occasion she invited students to her home for afternoon tea. She also received detailed reports from the students about the content of their instruction.

At one point, Nightingale concluded that the ward sisters [senior nurses] were not always adequately teaching the students. She agonized over the matter and, after considering it carefully, composed a "Memorandum of Instructions to Ward Sisters on Their Duties to Probationers [Student Nurses]." Though she couldn't physically be at the school, she worked diligently behind the scenes to ensure that it stayed on track as a school dedicated to its students.

From 1872, she began to write addresses to the students and graduates of the nursing school. In them, she repeatedly emphasized the importance of making continual progress. She wrote: "For us who Nurse, our Nursing is a thing, which, unless in it we are making *progress* every year, every month, every week, take my word for it we are going *back*. . . . Every year of her service a good Nurse will say: 'I learn something every day.'"[9] And she declared: "If you don't go on you will fall back. Aim higher."[10]

We mustn't compare ourselves to others. What is important is that we strive to be better today than we were yesterday and better tomorrow than we are today—that we advance, even if by only a single step, a single millimeter. Not advancing is regressing. As Nichiren Daishonin says in this famous passage: "Strengthen your faith day by day and month after month. Should you slacken in your resolve even a bit, devils will take advantage" (WND, p. 997).

Looking toward their futures in which they would take on positions of responsibility, Nightingale also warned the students against developing negative character traits such as selfishness, conceit, frivolity, vanity, temper, self-indulgence and lack of purpose.[11] People with these faults, she said, are unequal to the strict demands of life and work, and in most cases they end up giving up on their chosen path. She strongly urged the students not to become such people.

Those who have abandoned faith and betrayed the Soka Gakkai display the same negative traits. The Daishonin denounced the ignoble spirit of those who backslide in faith, calling them "cowardly, unreasoning, greedy, and doubting" (WND, 998).

chapter 6

FLORENCE NIGHTINGALE imparted many words of wisdom to the students of her training school for nurses. The graduates went out into the world with these precious gifts clasped to their hearts. For example, she wrote to them: "Training is enabling you to use the means you have in yourselves"[1]; "Remember, in little things as in great—No Cross [i.e., tribulations], [then] no Crown"[2]; and "What is our one thing needful? To have high principles at the bottom of all."[3]

Eventually, graduates of the Nightingale Training School for Nurses came to be matrons and ward sisters [head nurses and senior nurses] at England's leading hospitals and convalescent homes. They contributed to the development of nursing in many medical facilities. Graduates also went to work at hospitals in the United States, Canada, India, Sweden, Germany and other nations—many of them going on to serve as head nurses and in other responsible positions.

Students Will Become Founders

Nightingale declared: "Let each Founder train as many in his or her spirit as he or she can. Then the pupils will in their turn be Founders also."[4] And just as she said, graduates of her school, striving as her successors, lived their lives according to the highest ideals in countries throughout the globe.

The same can be said for the fine example of the graduates of the Soka School System (kindergarten through senior high school) and Soka University, who are active around the world. I understand Nightingale's feelings as she watched over her beloved "daughters" making wonderful contributions to society— happy for them as if they were her own children. She closely concerned herself with their welfare—Were they well? Were they working too hard? Were they eating properly?

When she heard that one of her graduates had fallen ill, she wrote out a dietary chart and sent it to her, along with money for food. She frequently sent graduates gifts of specialized medical texts or works of literature. Her concern even extended to the nurses working under the supervision of her graduates.

The graduates of her school in turn loved, respected and looked up to Nightingale as their model. They told her they were glad to have become her "daughters." Whenever they were facing some difficulty or a problem arose, they went to consult with her and ask for guidance. She always welcomed these visits. As she wrote to one of her protégés, "Your trials shall always be my trials, dear 'Little Sister.'"[5] This was her spirit as a mentor.

Every graduate who came and talked to her, without exception, felt as if their problems had disappeared, as if they were better and braver than before. Burning with hope again, they joyfully went back to their individual struggles. To her graduates, Nightingale was a safe harbor to return to. A person who possesses a "spiritual home port" is fortunate indeed.

Nothing great can be accomplished without fostering capable people; there can be no lasting victory. Nightingale knew this well. I can deeply relate to her fervent wish to leave behind even just one genuine successor. She risked her life to open the path for nurses, and countless successors followed in her wake. Many men were also among them.

Nursing and care for the elderly are a focus of increasing concern in our graying societies. I regard those who are engaged in the venerable work of relieving suffering and imparting joy as "great artists of healing," shining with intelligence, skill and character. We will only begin to see the emergence of truly "healthy" societies around the world when these noble caregivers are deeply respected and valued.

Learning to the Last Hour of Our Life

Nightingale promised her graduates: "I would try to be learning every day to the last hour of my life.... When I could no longer learn by nursing others, I would learn by being nursed, by seeing Nurses practise upon *me*."[6] And she was true to those words all her life.

At around age 40, when she founded the Nightingale Training School for Nurses, she suffered another serious decline in health. She was constantly afflicted with headaches, nausea and asthma attacks. Speaking for extended periods exhausted her. Many were worried that she might die an early death, and in fact she did face several health crises. Still, she never stopped her activities. She dismissed her illness, saying, "I am so busy that I have no time to die."[7]

Even though she couldn't get about freely, she could write letters. For that reason, she always kept a supply of pens and pencils by her bedside. She produced an enormous number of articles and statistical lists, as well as more than 12,000 letters. Though her doctor advised her to stop writing, this only spurred her on: "They say I must not write letters. Whereupon I do it all the more."[8] She also declared, "Had I 'lost' the Report [i.e., not been able to complete it], what would the health I should have 'saved' have profited me?"[9] These words illustrate the firm conviction that permeated her entire life. Nightingale was fueled by the

bright flame of a powerful inner purpose to which she gave herself unstintingly.

Eventually, Nightingale's sight began to fail, yet she declared: "No, no, a thousand times no. I am not growing apathetic."[10] In her early 80s, she went blind. Nevertheless, she did not despair. She kept going with the spirit that she still had ears to hear and a mouth to speak with. She astonished her visitors by how well abreast she was of current events.

The Buddhist sutras teach us that even if we lose our hands, we have our feet; even if we lose our feet, we have our eyes; even if we lose our eyes, we have our voice; even if we lose our voice, we have our life. With that resolve, we must spread Buddhism as long as we live. This is the spirit of a true Buddhist.

Even when Shakyamuni Buddha was on his deathbed, he preached the Law to an ascetic who had come to see him; he converted the man and welcomed him as his last disciple in his lifetime.

Josei Toda used to say that whether one's life was happy or unhappy was not decided until one's final years. The last years of Nightingale's life were the most beautiful and rich of all. She herself described her final years as the best days of her life. No woman was as loved and esteemed as she was at that time. It was said that just hearing her name mentioned cheered people up, and many women proclaimed that they wanted to be like her. People came from all over Britain and the world for her guidance and advice. Royalty and political leaders vied to meet her, but she refused to see anyone who did not have an interest in nursing.

She valued young people, saying, "All the more I am eager to see successors."[11] She received hundreds of letters from young girls who wanted to be nurses, and she answered most of them. To the very end, she sought out and challenged things that needed doing, planting the seeds of the future: "To make an art of *Life!* That is the finest art of all the Fine Arts."[12] And that is precisely how Nightingale lived hers.

On August 13, 1910, that "artful life" came quietly to a close.

She was 90 years old, and it was in the year marking the fiftieth anniversary of her school's founding. In accord with her wishes, her funeral was simple.

Nightingale viewed death as the beginning of a fresh round of "*immense* activity."[13] Nichiren Daishonin writes, "We repeat the cycle of birth and death secure upon the great earth of our intrinsically enlightened nature" (*Gosho Zenshu*, p. 724). Those who have faith in the Mystic Law advance with joy in both life and death on the great earth of their intrinsically enlightened nature—in other words, the earth of Buddhahood.

Life is eternal. That is why it is essential to forge an absolutely indestructible life-state of eternity, happiness, true self and purity in this existence. To do that, we need correct faith, and equally essential are sincere and just actions for the sake of others. Those who devote their lives to kosen-rufu can walk the path of eternal happiness savoring the highest of all joys.

A New Century of Women

In the last address to the students at her school, written in 1900, when she was 80 years old, Nightingale spoke of "the century of Woman." These were to be her last public words. In the address she wrote: "The 19th century (there was the tradition) was to be [the] century of Woman. How true that legendary prophesy has been! Woman was the home drudge. Now she is the teacher."[14]

In the new Century of Women, the twenty-first century, women will lead the way for society.

Some fifty years earlier, in 1851, Nightingale had declared that it was women themselves, by failing to take action, who hindered the arrival of an age of women. She was 30 at the time and had at last found her vocation in nursing. She undoubtedly looked forward to the arrival of an age when women would be empowered rather than dependent and when they would act with purpose and courage for society and humanity.

Today, the SGI women's and young women's divisions members—especially the nurses' group members, the Nightingales of the Mystic Law—are advancing in the vanguard of the century of women.

I have an unforgettable personal memory related to Nightingale. It took place soon after I started practicing Nichiren Daishonin's Buddhism in 1947. I was attending one of President Toda's lectures on the Lotus Sutra. The lecture had ended and we were engaging in a question-and-answer session. A member of the young women's division asked Mr. Toda: "There are many fine people who do not practice this Buddhism. How should we view this?"

Mr. Toda replied with warmth and at the same time firmness: "Yes, that's true. And perhaps compared to those 'fine people' you may seem to be just an ordinary woman. But you uphold the great teaching of the Mystic Law. This is a wonderful thing. Upholding the Mystic Law and teaching it to others, devoting one's life to kosen-rufu is the finest life any woman can lead."

He continued: "You may not be able to compare to Florence Nightingale, who achieved so many great things and left a brilliant record of accomplishments. Nor do you have to. But your spirit and determination should never be inferior to hers."

Mr. Toda's words were clear-cut, strict yet compassionate. I can still hear that guidance ringing in my ears.

Nightingale gave her life to nursing. It was a life that demonstrated to future generations the incredible strength and capacity of a person who is fully awakened to their life's mission as they fight their way valiantly through the crushing breakers of adversity to reach their goal. Let us live that kind of life, too. Say to the world: "Watch and see what I will achieve in 10 years, in 50!" "Look at this life dedicated to kosen-rufu!" And send the light of courage to people everywhere.

Nichiren Daishonin writes, "Of all medicines, Nam-myoho-renge-kyo is the best medicine" (*Gosho Zenshu,* p. 335). From the fundamental aspect of life itself, the Mystic Law is the "wonderful medicine," the "highly efficient medicine" that heals, revitalizes and relieves human beings of suffering. In your devotion to the Mystic Law and your efforts to widely share the Mystic Law with others, you are the greatest and most respectworthy "doctors of life," "nurses of life."

Let us proudly and courageously engage in wide "life-revitalizing" dialogue. Acting as a beacon of hope, please guide others on a sure course through the rough seas of society and create countless "silver waves of transforming destiny" and "golden waves of human revolution" throughout the world.

e n d n o t e s

Chapter 1

1. Cecil Woodham-Smith, *Florence Nightingale* (London: Constable and Company, Ltd., 1951), 13.

2. Ibid., 44.

3. Elspeth Huxley, *Florence Nightingale* (London: Weidenfeld and Nicolson, 1975), 38.

4. Ibid.

5. Sir Edward Cook, *The Life of Florence Nightingale* (London: Macmillan and Co., Ltd., 1913), vol. 1, 63.

6. Ibid., 82.

7. Ibid., 106.

8. Ibid., 54.

9. Woodham-Smith, *Florence Nightingale*, 83.

Chapter 2

1. Woodham-Smith, *Florence Nightingale*, 88.

2. Huxley, *Florence Nightingale*, 42.

3. Florence Nightingale, *Notes on Nursing: What It Is, and What It Is Not* (New York: Dover Publications, Inc., 1969), 135.

4. Florence Nightingale, *Notes on Nursing: What It Is, and What It Is Not,* new edition, revised and enlarged (London: Harrison, 1860), 198.

5. Ibid., 199.

6. Shrimala: A daughter of King Prasenajit of Kosala in the days of Shakyamuni and the wife of the king of Ayodhya. She was extremely wise and had deep faith in Buddhism, and she and her husband converted many people. Shrimala is said to have expounded the *Shoman* or Shrimala Sutra with the help of the Buddha's power.

7. *The Lion's Roar of Queen Srimala Sutra,* translated by Alex and Hideko Wayman (New York: Columbia University Press, 1974), chap. 1.

8. Florence Nightingale, "Sick-Nursing and Health-Nursing," *Selected Writings of Florence Nightingale,* compiled by Lucy Ridgely Seymer (New York: Macmillan Company, 1954), 364.

9. Cook, *The Life of Florence Nightingale*, vol. 2, 434.

Chapter 3

1. Woodham-Smith, *Florence Nightingale*, 139.

2. Ibid., 207.

3. Cook, *The Life of Florence Nightingale*, vol. 2, 413.

4. Ibid., vol. 1, 237.

5. Nightingale, *Notes on Nursing: What It Is, and What It Is Not*, 42.

6. Cook, vol. 1, xxiii.

7. Woodham-Smith, *Florence Nightingale*, 200.

8. Ibid., 209.

9. Ibid., 232.

10. Tsunesaburo Makiguchi, *Makiguchi Tsunesaburo Zenshu* (The Collected Works of Tsunesaburo Makiguchi), vol. 6, 71.

11. Woodham-Smith, *Florence Nightingale*, 231.

12. Florence Nightingale, *As Miss Nightingale Said...*, edited by Monica Baly (London: Scutari Press, 1991), 33.

Chapter 4

1. Cook, *The Life of Florence Nightingale*, vol. 1, 268.

2. Woodham-Smith, *Florence Nightingale*, 259.

3. Woodham-Smith, *Florence Nightingale*, 270.

4. Florence Nightingale, Address dated New Year's Day, 1878. Manuscript kept at the Florence Nightingale Museum, St. Thomas' Hospital in London.

5. Nightingale, *Notes on Nursing: What It Is, and What It Is Not*, 7.

Chapter 5

1. Nightingale, *Notes on Nursing: What It Is, and What It Is Not*, 8.

2. Ibid.

3. Florence Nightingale, "Training of Nurses and Nursing the Sick," from *Selected Writings of Florence Nightingale*, compiled by Lucy Ridgely Seymer, 335.

4. Florence Nightingale, *Notes on Hospitals* (London: Longman, Green, Longman, Roberts, and Green, 1863), iii.

5. H.R.H. the Prince of Wales, *A Vision of Britain: A Personal View of Architecture* (London: Doubleday, 1989), 117.

6. Ibid.

7. Woodham-Smith, *Florence Nightingale*, 339.

8. Cook, *The Life of Florence Nightingale*, vol. 1, 461.

9. Florence Nightingale, Address dated May 1872, in *Florence Nightingale to Her Nurses* (London: Macmillan and Co., Limited, 1914), 1-2.

10. Florence Nightingale, Address dated May 23, 1883. Manuscript kept at the Florence Nightingale Museum, St. Thomas' Hospital in London.

11. Nightingale, Address dated May 1872, in *Florence Nightingale to Her Nurses*, 19.

Chapter 6

1. Nightingale, Address dated May 23, 1883.

2. Nightingale, Address dated April 28, 1876, in *Florence Nightingale to Her Nurses*, 116.

3. Ibid., 90. Address dated May 26, 1875.

4. Cook, *The Life of Florence Nightingale*, vol. 2, 246.

5. Ibid., vol. 2, 260.

6. Nightingale, Address dated May 1872, in *Florence Nightingale to Her Nurses*, 2.

7. Zachary Cope, *Florence Nightingale and the Doctors* (Philadelphia and Montreal: J.B. Lippincott Company, 1958), 37.

8. Woodham-Smith, *Florence Nightingale*, 387.

9. Ibid., 300.

10. Ibid., 589.

11. Ibid., 585-86.

12. Cook, *The Life of Florence Nightingale*, vol. 2, 430.

13. Ibid., vol. 2, 402.

14. Florence Nightingale, Address dated May 28, 1900. Manuscript kept at the Department of Manuscripts, the British Library in London.